SLAM DUNK

JOKES
For Kids!

BOB PHILLIPS

HARVEST HOUSE PUBLISHERS

EUGENE, OREGON

All Scripture references in this book are taken from the King James Version of the Bible.

Cover by Terry Dugan Design, Minneapolis, Minnesota

Illustrations by Harvest House Publishers, Katie Brady

SLAM DUNK JOKES FOR KIDS
Copyright © 2004 by Bob Phillips
Published by Harvest House Publishers
Eugene, Oregon 97402

ISBN 0-7369-1346-7

Printed in the United States of America

04 05 06 07 08 09 10 11 /BC-KB/ 10 9 8 7 6 5 4 3 2 1

Contents

Contents

1

Basketball

A basketball coach discovered a college basketball player was a dream come true. He was 7'4" tall and never missed a basket. The problem was that he was not too bright. He didn't do well in school.

The coach begged the academic dean to let the young man play ball. The dean said, "If he can answer three questions correctly, I will let him play."

The basketball player was brought before the dean. The dean said, "How much is two and two?"

The young man thought and thought and finally said, "Four."

The dean asked the second question. "How much is four plus four?"

The young man gulped, made faces, and finally said, "Eight."

The dean asked the last question. "How much is eight plus eight?"

Beads of sweat formed on the young man's forehead. After a long pause he said, "Sixteen."

With that the coach yelled and fell to his knees before the dean and said, "Please, Dean, give him one more chance."

1st sports fan: I hear they are feeding basketball players monkeys' favorite food—bananas—before each game.

2nd sports fan: Does it make them shoot any better?

1st sports fan: Not really, but you should see them swing from the basketball hoops.

Slam Dunk Amazing Fact

On April 6, 1935, at 7:00 in the evening, 4,000 basketball fans went to the Madison Street Armory in Chicago. They went to see a man by the name of Harold (Bunny) Levitt.

These fans witnessed Bunny throw 499 free throws without missing. He tossed the ball underhanded with both hands. It was a little before midnight when Bunny missed his 500th throw.

Most of the crowd went home but Bunny stayed until 2:30 in the morning. He tossed another 371 shots without missing.

Later, Bunny joined the Harlem Globetrotters. The Globetrotters offered $1,000 to any man who could beat Bunny in a contest of 100 free-throw shots. No one ever beat him.

Harold (Bunny) Levitt never became a big name in basketball and he never played on any major teams. He had a handicap that made it difficult for him to play against other basketball players—Bunny was only 5'4" inches tall.

Why was Cinderella such a terrible basketball player?

Because she had a pumpkin for a coach.

Did you hear about one basketball player who
negotiated his own professional contract for
10 million dollars?

He got ten dollars a year for a million years.

Why did all of the basketball players hold their
noses?

Because one player was making a foul shot.

The biggest trouble with referees is that
they don't care who wins.

What is a personal foul?

Having your very own chicken.

—Slam Dunk Amazing Fact—

Paul Anderson was the first man in recorded history to (cold press) lift 400 pounds from the floor to above his head. He went on to lift a table off of the floor that had weight on it that totaled 6,270 pounds.

Reporter: Coach, what do you have to say about losing so many games?

Coach: Well, there is good news and bad news.

Reporter: What is the bad news?

Coach: We lost 15 games in a row.

Reporter: What is the good news?

Coach: We're on a one-game winning streak.

Dottie: What disease makes you a better basketball player?

Ignatius: I have no idea.

Dottie: Athlete's foot.

What dessert is not good for basketball players to eat?
Turnovers.

Dork: What do they call a chicken who keeps missing free throws in a basketball game?
Mork: I give.
Dork: A foul up.

How do they play basketball in Hawaii?
With hula hoops.

Christy: What would you get if you crossed a newborn snake with a basketball?
Lisa: I have no idea.
Christy: A bouncing baby boa.

──Slam Dunk Amazing Fact──

On July 25, 1940, John Sigmund entered the Mississippi River at St. Louis, Missouri. He began swimming and continued for 89 hours and 46 minutes.

His wife Catherine furnished him with candy bars for energy and encouraged him onward.

After he emerged from the water, he could not stand up. His friends had to carry him. He had covered the distance of 292 miles.

When is a basketball player like a baby?
When he dribbles.

Is it true that basketball is a dance held in a basket?

I'll give you an idea how smart our basketball team is. The other weekend we were in a bus on the way to play a game. All of a sudden the bus driver slammed on the brakes and yelled, "Look at that pig with one eye." Quickly, the entire team covered one eye and looked.

A cheerleader said to one of the basketball players, "You smell good. What do you have on?" The basketball player replied, "Clean socks."

Our basketball team was so bad that when one of the players hit the rim, everyone gave him high fives.

Why did the bench-sitter take a water gun to the basketball game?

He wanted a chance to shoot the ball.

──Slam Dunk Amazing Fact──

February 21, 1882—James Saunders ran 120 miles in less than 24 hours.

A coach wanted to give his team a pep talk after losing the game. He said, "We need to get back to the basics of the game."

With that, he picked up the ball and said, "This is a basketball."

One of the players said, "Not so fast, Coach."

Why does it get hot after a basketball game?
Because all the fans are gone.

Our basketball team was so bad that when we came on the court, our manager received a fine for littering.

What do pigs do when they play basketball?
They hog the ball.

Reporter: What is the bigger problem for an
    NBA player—ignorance or apathy?
Coach: I don't know and I don't care.

Reporter: Do you have a fight song for your
    basketball team?
Coach: All we have is a surrender song.

—Slam Dunk Amazing Fact—

July 10, 1924—Paavo Nurmi won two
Olympic distance races in 1 day—1,500 m. and
5,000 m.

Why did the ticket seller at the basketball game let the chicken in? Also, why did he let the turkey, the pheasant, and the goose come in, but turn away the duck?

Because at a basketball game—five fowls and you're out.

Lisa: How many players does it take to shoot a basketball?

Linus: I'm blank.

Lisa: Two. One to throw the ball and the other to fire the shotgun.

Our basketball team was really tough. They gave us lots of names like Scarface, Blackie, Toothless, and Bad Breath—and that was just the cheerleaders.

I don't want to say that the referees were blind or dumb—but if you put the brains of three officials into a hummingbird, it would just fly backward.

What team is known for traveling with the ball?
The Harlem Globetrotters.

Basketball player: We're going to win this game—don't you think so, coach?
Coach: I certainly hoop so.

──Slam Dunk Amazing Fact──

May 1, 1929—Johnny Finn hopped 100 yards in a sack race in 14.4 seconds.

I don't want to say that our seats are up very high in the stadium—but the stewardess strapped me into mine before the game.

Basketball fan: What your team needs is more shooters.

Coach: No, we have enough shooters. What we really need is makers.

Did you hear about the basketball team for those over fifty years of age? They don't use jump balls. The referee just puts the ball on the floor, and whoever can bend over and pick it up gets possession.

I knew it was going to be a wild basketball game when a fight broke out in the middle of the national anthem.

Why did the retired basketball player become a judge?
He wanted to stay on the court.

Delbert: Why did the chicken cross the basketball court?
Darlene: I have no clue.
Delbert: Because the referee called a fowl.

How did the basketball court get wet?
The players dribbled all over it.

Reporter: Coach, what do you have to say about your basketball team losing so many games?

Coach: Well, the preseason predictions were correct. They said we were the team to beat—and everybody did.

2

Cheerleaders

Wilson: I had a friend who was cheerleader
  for the golf team.

Arnold: I've never heard of such a thing.

Wilson: His job was to go around, going "Sh-Sh."

Knock, knock.
Who's there?
Ice cream.
Ice cream who?
Ice cream because I'm one of the cheerleaders.

Our team was so bad that we had to rent cheerleaders.

─Slam Dunk Amazing Fact─

February 21, 1983—Donald Davis ran the fastest backward mile in 6 minutes and 7.1 seconds.

Alfreda: How do loudmouths pay for college?
Amelia: I have no idea.
Alfreda: They get hollerships.

What is a cheerleader's favorite drink?
Root beer.

What is a cheerleader's favorite color?
Yeller.

Our team is so bad the cheerleaders stay home and just e-mail their cheers.

3

Tennis

Alec: I know everything there is to know about tennis.

Alma: Okay—how many holes are there in a tennis net?

Hubert: What can you serve but not eat?

Erastus: I have no idea.

Hubert: A tennis ball.

Quentin: What do you call a teacher with a
   tennis racket on her head?

Quimby: You tell me.

Quentin: Annette.

Discussing his tennis technique, a stout, bald
man panted: "My brain immediately barks out a
command to my body. 'Run forward, and fast,' it
says. 'Start right now. Drop the ball gracefully
over the net and walk back slowly.'"

"And then what happens?" asked a friend.

"And then my body asks, 'Who, me?'"

—Slam Dunk Amazing Fact—

April 25, 1999 to January 25, 2000—Gary
Parsons ran 11,824.8 miles in 274 days.

Petula: Why is tennis such a noisy game?
Olaf: You tell me.
Petula: Because each player raises a racket.

Quentin: What number and letter describe a popular outdoor game?
Quimby: I haven't got a clue.
Quentin: 10 S.

Mavis: Where is tennis mentioned in the Bible?
Mable: You've got me.
Mavis: When Joseph served in Pharaoh's court.

Sign in the window of a sporting goods store: SALE ON TENNIS BALLS. FIRST COME, FIRST SERVE.

4

Wrestling

1st wrestler: I hear you are taking a mail-order bodybuilding course.

2nd wrestler: You're right. Every week, the mailman brings me a new piece of body-building equipment.

1st wrestler: You don't look any different to me.

2nd wrestler: You're right—but you should see my mailman.

1st wrestler: Want to see something really swell?

2nd wrestler: Sure.

1st wrestler: Hit yourself on the head with a baseball bat.

—Slam Dunk Amazing Fact—

Do you like to do sit-ups? Well, Marine captain Wayne E. Rollings did. On September 13, 1971, the captain began to do his sit-ups. He continued for 7 hours and 27 minutes to complete 17,000 sit-ups.

On August 17, 1974, another Marine captain, Alan Jones, set the record in doing 27,003 sit-ups in 30 hours. What makes this such an achievement was the fact Captain Jones had polio when he was a child. This was later followed by a back injury. The doctors told him he would never do any heavy lifting.

5

Scrambled Sports

Here's a scramble with letters to sort. The right answer is a type of sport.

Sorcs-rynutco nsikig

Here's a scramble with letters to sort. The right answer is a type of sport.

Ismwgnim

Here's a scramble with letters to sort. The right answer is a type of sport.

Sheohsroes

Here's a scramble with letters to sort. The right answer is a type of sport.

Tkrca nda lefid

Here's a scramble with letters to sort. The right answer is a type of sport.

Ghweit gliiftn

Here's a scramble with letters to sort. The right answer is a type of sport.

Ngfenci

─Slam Dunk Amazing Fact─

Who invented the game of baseball as we know it today? Most people would say Abner Doubleday. However, the man who standard-ized the game as we know it was Alexander Cartwright.

Cartwright made the baseball field into a diamond shape. He set the bases 90 feet apart, and named the fourth base "home." He also established "three strikes and you're out."

Here's a scramble with letters to sort. The right answer is a type of sport.

Logf

Here's a scramble with letters to sort. The right answer is a type of sport.

Gihh mupijng

Here's a scramble with letters to sort. The right answer is a type of sport.

Derdnuh dyar sahd

Here's a scramble with letters to sort. The right answer is a type of sport.

Tsoh upt

6

That's Sporting

What do you get when you cross a computer
with a track-and-field star?

A floppy discus thrower.

Why is a karate blow like a piece of meat?

Because it is a poke chop.

My team has been in the cellar so long, our team mascot is a mushroom.

Rudolf: What's the hardest foot to buy a
   roller skate for?
Wilbur: I give up.
Rudolf: A square foot.

Willy: Where do biologists like to go for swim
   class?
Hermon: You've got me.
Willy: In the gene pool.

Reporter: Coach, how do you feel after losing
   the game?
Coach: I feel like the guy in the javelin
   competition who won the toss and elected
   to receive.

Jeff: What do you call a knight who just lost a fencing match?

Nole: You tell me.

Jeff: A sword loser.

Why did the boy keep his racing bicycle in his bedroom?

He was tired of walking in his sleep.

Next to hockey and soccer, what is the most shin-bruising game in America?

Bridge.

Gideon: What do you get if you tie two racing
  bicycles together?

Gloria: I have no idea.

Gideon: Siamese Schwinns.

Jon-Mark: What animal has two trunks and
  swims in the Olympics?

Julius: You've got me.

Jon-Mark: An elephant.

—Slam Dunk Amazing Fact—

Ty Cobb retired in 1928 with 4,191 hits.
His nickname was the "Georgia Peach."

A racehorse can take several thousand
people for a ride at the same time.

Myrtle: Who makes the world's greatest milk-
shake?
Maynard: Who knows?
Myrtle: A cow on a trampoline.

What's the best place to shop for a soccer
shirt?
New Jersey.

Teacher: Johnny, name the four seasons.
Johnny: Football, basketball, baseball, and
soccer.

1st fan: I can tell you what the score's going
to be before this game starts.
2nd fan: Really, what is it?
1st fan: Nothing to nothing.

Slam Dunk Amazing Fact

> Do you like hot dogs at a baseball game?
> The first hot dog was sold by Harry M. Stevens
> in 1901 at the Polo Grounds in New York City.

Where in the Bible does it say that we should
not play marbles?
*In John 3:7—Jesus said to Nicodemus, "Marvel
not..." [Marble-not]*

My sports career ended abruptly. My team
retired my jersey while I was still in it.

Lady at the store: I am a physical education
    teacher and I would like to buy a pair of
    shorts to wear around my gymnasium.
Clerk: Well, how big is your gymnasium?

I think my days on the team are numbered.
I was recently sent on a scouting trip to the
Bermuda Triangle.

No one laughed when I fell while ice
skating—but the ice made some awful cracks.

Where do religious kids practice sports?
On the prayground.

Slam Dunk Amazing Fact

Did you know that college football has been played for more than 130 years?

George: What is badmutton?

Mabel: I think it is a game played with a butcher.

Boy: I don't think the fellas on the archery team like me.

Mother: Why do you say that?

Boy: They asked me to join the archery team as the wide receiver.

What do you get if you cross a karate expert with a tree?

Spruce Lee.

Igor: What do you do to a bad Ping-Pong ball?
Theda: I have no clue.
Igor: Paddle it.

Did you hear the radio announcer give the latest
   football scores?

   The Lions devoured the Saints.

   The Vikings clobbered the Dolphins.

   The Falcons tore the Cardinals to shreds.

   The Broncos trampled the Rams.

   The Bears mauled the Buccaneers.

   The Giants squashed the Packers.

   The Jets shot down the Eagles.

   The Bengals chewed up the Colts.

─Slam Dunk Amazing Fact─

Dr. James Naismith invented the game of basketball. It started when he nailed a basket to the balcony in a YMCA gym. The balls he used were soccer balls. The first game was played in 1891. The game is now played in 150 countries around the world.

During a Ping-Pong game, one of the contestants accidentally swallowed the ball. The ambulance came and sped him to the hospital, where he was quickly rushed into the operating room.

When he recovered after the operation, he noticed a dozen scars all over his body—some on his chest and some on his stomach. "Why did you cut me in so many places?" he asked the doctor.

The surgeon answered, "That's just the way the ball bounces."

7

Running

Tyler: Why do fast-food lovers do so well in marathons?

Ryan: You tell me.

Tyler: They like to eat and run.

Mavis: What do you do if you split your sides laughing?

Mable: Who knows?

Mavis: Start running until you get a stitch in your side.

Norm: What's the best way to describe an out-of-shape marathoner?

Nancy: You've got me guessing.

Norm: A sore loser.

After hearing the story about how God took the rib out of Adam's side, a little boy who had been running and had a side ache said to his mother, "I think I'm going to have a wife."

Quentin: What is the best thing for a runner to eat before a race?

Quimby: I have no idea.

Quentin: Ketchup.

Slam Dunk Amazing Fact

Why do we call a 26-mile (385 yard) race a marathon? It all began back in September of 490 B.C. King Darius, the ruler of the Persian Empire, sent his army to attack the city-state of Athens. The battle took place on the plains of Marathon, not far from Athens.

It looked like the Athenians would lose the battle. They needed help. They chose a man named Pheidippides to run to the city of Sparta to get help from their allies. He was their fastest runner.

Pheidippides ran all day and through the night on a very difficult road, 140 miles to Sparta. He delivered the message and ran back to join his fellow soldiers. He had covered a distance of 280 miles in about 48 hours. He then helped to fight in the battle and the Persians were defeated.

The leaders wanted the news of the victory to get back to the citizens of Athens. Pheidippides threw off his heavy armor and ran 22 miles to Athens with the message.

Pheidippides ran the distance in just a few hours...but his body was worn out by his previous running and fighting. He ran into the central marketplace shouting, "Victory! Victory!" Then he collapsed and died. The Athenians never forgot his courage, patriotism, and sacrifice. The people established a series of games in his honor. In 1896, the long-distance road race in the Olympics was named the marathon.

Reporter: How long have you been running?
Track Star: Since I was ten years old.
Reporter: You sure must be tired.

Did you hear about the cross-eyed runner who was also a discus thrower? He wasn't that good, but he sure kept the crowd alert.

Hobart: What ancient Egyptian beauty queen wore spiked running shoes?
Herman: Beats me.
Hobart: Cleats-o-patra.

──**Slam Dunk Amazing Fact**──

Have you ever wondered why tennis balls are fuzzy? It helps slow the ball down by creating wind resistance.

8

Boxing

Did you hear about the boxer who was knocked out so many times they sold advertising on the soles of his shoes?

Did you hear the joke about a boxer? It'll knock you out.

Did you hear about the boxer who had the following written on his tombstone: You can stop counting. I'm not getting up.

Boxing coach: You did a terrible job out there. If I were as big as you, I would be heavy-weight champion of the world.

Boxer: Then, why don't you get into the ring and become the lightweight champion of the world?

He really isn't a very good boxer. In fact, he is the only boxer in the history of the sport to be knocked out while shadow boxing.

There was a fighter who was taking a terrible beating. He was losing the fight. When the bell rang, he staggered to his corner. His manager said to him, "I think you had better let him hit you with his right for a while. Your face is crooked."

Reporter to Boxing Champ: What is your best punch?

Boxing Champ: I don't know. I never hit myself.

Rufus: What food can never become the heavyweight champion of the world?

Maynard: I don't know.

Rufus: A lollipop. It always gets licked.

Nit: Why did the prizefighter like his new
    job?
Wit: I have no idea.
Nit: He got to punch the time clock.

Ken: What are a boxer's favorite colors?
Bob: I couldn't guess.
Ken: Black and blue.

Boxer: Have I done any damage to the other
    boxer?
Trainer: No, but keep swinging. The draft
    might give him a cold.

Have you ever seen a shoe box?

Isaac: What dog stands the best chance of winning the heavyweight title?

Isabel: I'm blank.

Isaac: A boxer, of course.

9

Skydiving

Instructor: What I want you to do—after jumping out of the plane—is to count to ten and then pull the rip cord.

Skydiver: W-w-w-w-w-w-whhhattt w-w-w-w-was th-th-th-that n-n-n-n-num-m-m-m-b-b-b-b-er?"

Instructor: Two!

Reporter: How did you take up skydiving?

Skydiver: It all started when I was a passenger on a plane that ran out of gas.

Skydiver: What do you want me to do?

Instructor: When you jump out of the plane, try and land on the little black spot on the ground.

Skydiver: Is that all I have to do?

Instructor: No, remember to pull the rip cord or the little black spot on the ground will be you.

Slam Dunk Amazing Fact

Lillian Leitzel was an acrobat with the Ringling Bros. and Barnum & Bailey Circus. She only weighed 95 pounds and stood 4'9" tall—but Lillian was strong.

At Hermann's Gym in Philadelphia, she said she could beat the record for one-handed chin-ups. The record was then held by an Englishman named Cutler who did 12 one-handed chin-ups.

Lillian jumped up to the bar with her right hand and proceeded to complete 27 one-armed chin-ups. After a short rest, she shocked the crowd by jumping up again to the bar and doing 19 one-armed chin-ups with her left hand.

10

Football

Why did the football coach send in his second string?

To tie up the game.

Customer: Do you sell football shoes?

Clerk: Why, yes, we do. What size is your football?

What should a fullback do when he gets a handoff?

Go to a secondhand store.

Knock, knock.
Who's there?
Justin.
Justin who?
You're Justin time for the kickoff.

Moe: Why did the football player complain to the waiter?

Joe: I don't have a clue.

Moe: Because there was a fly in his soup-er bowl.

Did you hear about the scandal at the University? Three football players were caught sneaking into the library.

Slam Dunk Amazing Fact

Roy Riegels is famous for his 70-yard football run. Roy was a defensive lineman for the University of California. The game was against Georgia Tech at the Rose Bowl in Pasadena, California. Georgia Tech fumbled the football and Roy Riegels picked it up and started running. Everyone in the stands leaped to their feet and started yelling. Roy was running the wrong way. A fellow teammate tackled him on his own one yard line. Georgia Tech won by the score of 8 to 7. It was not a good day for "Wrong Way" Riegels.

Thelma: Why are football stadiums so cold?
Anita: I don't have the foggiest.
Thelma: Because they have too many fans.

Our football team was so bad that our homecoming was scheduled as an away game.

Mike: I once was a football player.

Spike: What position did you play, fullback?

Mike: Nope.

Spike: Did you play halfback?

Mike: Nope.

Spike: What position did you play?

Mike: Drawback.

Willard: Why do you think football is such a rough sport?

Brenda: That's a tough question to tackle.

Why did the football player do a commercial for hair shampoo?

He was having trouble with split ends.

─Slam Dunk Amazing Fact─

Jean Behra was a famous French race-car driver. He lost his ear in a racing crash. He now wears a plastic ear, and he keeps a spare one in his pocket.

A star football player was told he would not be able to play because he failed his math test. The coach begged the math teacher to let the star player make up the test. The math teacher said, "Okay."

Later the coach saw the math teacher and asked, "How did Wilconski do?"

"I'm sorry to say that he failed. I asked him what 5 times 8 was. He said, 38."

"Give him a break," pleaded the coach. "He only missed it by one."

Boy: Doctor, do you think I can play football after this cast is off my leg?

Doctor: Certainly, young man.

Boy: Thanks. I couldn't play before.

1st football wife: When my husband dies, I'm not going to have him buried.

2nd football wife: What are you going to do?

1st football wife: I'm going to have him stuffed and mounted. Then I am going to put him on the living room couch and turn on a football game. I will talk to him—and of course he won't answer. It will be just like he never left.

Football player: Coach, my doctor says I can't play football.

Coach: You didn't have to go to a doctor. I could have told you that.

—Slam Dunk Amazing Fact—

The great baseball hitter, Babe Ruth, hit 714 home runs. He held the record for many years. He also holds the record for the most strike outs—1,330.

What do you call the football player who guesses the other team's plays?

The hunchback.

Why shouldn't you borrow a penny from a football coach?

Because he always wants a quarter back.

Did you hear about the coach who got mad at the referee? He ran out on the field and said to the referee, "You stink!"

The referee then picked up the football and paced off an additional 15 yards. He then turned and looked at the coach and said, "Okay, how do I smell from here?"

Geraldine: Who are the most despised football players?

Gaspar: Beats me.

Geraldine: The offensive team.

I don't want to say our lineman was dumb, but he once got lost in a huddle.

—Slam Dunk Amazing Fact—

Did you know that a field goal in football happens very quickly? The snap, reception, placement, and kick takes about 1.05 seconds.

Husband to wife: "Hey, Gladis, do you have
   anything to say to me before football
   season starts?"

What do you call it when your toes have a good
   cry?
Footbawl.

Did you hear about the football player who
injured himself? His coach told him to go in and
run around his own end.

Church member: Pastor, do you like football?
Pastor: Why, yes, I do. I even have a football
   theology.
Church member: What is that?

Pastor: Well, a draft choice is the pew that's not too close to the air-conditioner. A bench-warmer is an inactive member. "In the pocket" is where too many people keep their offering. A fumble is a lousy sermon. And the two-minute warning happens when the deacon in the front row takes a peek at his watch and makes sure I see it.

11

Fishing

Two fishermen were out fishing on a large lake. One of them caught a very large bass.

"We should mark this spot. It is a good place to catch fish," said the man who caught the bass. The other man then drew a large X on the side of the boat.

"That won't do any good," said the man who caught the fish.

"Why not?" said the man who made the X.

"Next time out, we may not get the same boat."

A young boy protested when his mother asked him to take his little sister fishing with him. "The last time I took her, I didn't catch a single fish."

"I'll tell her to keep quiet while you are fishing," said his mother. "She won't make any noise."

"It wasn't the noise, Mom," replied the boy. "She ate all my worms."

How do not-so-smart fishermen count their daily catch of fish?

One fish...two fish...another fish...another fish... another fish.

Why are fishermen and shepherds not to be trusted?

Because they live by hook and by crook.

──Slam Dunk Amazing Fact──

Who has scored the most points in the game of soccer? His name is Edson Arantes do Nascimento from Brazil. He scored 1,281 goals in the 1,363 games of his career. By the way, he is also known as the world-famous Pelé.

If you think that fishermen are the biggest liars in the world, just ask a jogger how many miles a day he runs.

"Would you go fishing with me?" Tom asked with baited breath.

Why couldn't Batman go fishing?
Robin ate all the worms.

Ichabod: What is the fastest fish in the water?

Ignatius: That's a mystery.

Ichabod: A motorpike.

How do fish go into business?
They start on a small scale.

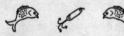

Slam Dunk Amazing Fact

The worst baseball catch was by American League catcher Joe Sprinz. He tried to catch baseballs that were dropped from a blimp 1,000 feet in the air.

Sprinz missed the first four balls. He did, however, catch the fifth ball. It was traveling so fast that it knocked his glove back into his face and he lost four teeth.

Why is it, whenever you go fishing, people will always ask, "Did you catch those fish?" What do they think—they just jumped in the boat and surrendered?

Three-fourths of the Earth's surface is water and one-fourth is land. It's obvious that the good Lord intended that man should spend three times as much time fishing as plowing.

Elton: What is a frog's favorite sport?
Erwin: I give up.
Elton: Fly-fishing.

12

Bowling

1st bowler: I know a girl who was asked to quit the bowling team—after knocking down all the pins every time she threw the bowling ball.

2nd bowler: That doesn't seem fair.

1st bowler: All of the pins were in the next alley.

Christy: What is the quietest game in the world?

Lisa: You've got me.

Christy: Bowling. You can hear a pin drop.

Interest your children in bowling. It's a great way to get them off the streets and into the alleys.

What do you do with old bowling balls?

Give them to the elephants to shoot as marbles.

Bertram: Which animal is the best athlete?

Bunsby: How should I know?

Bertram: The bowler bear.

─Slam Dunk Amazing Fact─

On July 2, 1970, Lyman Dickinson bowled a 299 point game—just one pin short of a perfect score of 300.

What made this such a feat was Lyman Dickinson had lost both of his legs to amputation. He bowled his 299 game while wearing his artificial legs.

In bowling, the bowler has to make a series of quick steps forward and then come to a complete stop. His feet must not cross the foul line.

It is amazing what a person can do once he applies courage, determination, and practice.

If our town didn't have bowling, there would be no culture at all.

One of the advantages of bowling over golf is that you very seldom lose a bowling ball.

What sport was once illegal in many states? That's right. You guessed it. Bowling.

A bowling alley is a place where pin pals meet.

13

Scrambled Sports

Here's a scramble with letters to sort. The right answer is a type of sport.

Idefl yekoch

Here's a scramble with letters to sort. The right answer is a type of sport.

Wginobl

Here's a scramble with letters to sort. The right answer is a type of sport.

Quorcet

Here's a scramble with letters to sort. The right answer is a type of sport.

Lloofabt

Here's a scramble with letters to sort. The right answer is a type of sport.

Oopl

Here's a scramble with letters to sort. The right answer is a type of sport.

Lldnahba

Slam Dunk Amazing Fact

The longest boxing match took place between Andy Bowen and Jack Burke in New Orleans. It started at 9:15 p.m. on April 7 and was finished on April 8 at 4:34 a.m. No one won the fight. It was called a draw after 110 rounds.

Here's a scramble with letters to sort. The right answer is a type of sport.

Xiobng

Here's a scramble with letters to sort. The right answer is a type of sport.

Tgilnrwes

Here's a scramble with letters to sort. The right answer is a type of sport.

Wsginimm

Here's a scramble with letters to sort. The right answer is a type of sport.

Klalbetsab

14

Baseball

Did you hear about the manager who walked out to the pitcher's mound and said to the pitcher, "You're through."

"But, coach," said the pitcher. "I struck this guy out last time."

"Yeah," said the manager, "But this is the same inning."

Knock, knock.
Who's there?
Philip.
Philip who?
Hit the ball and Philip the bases.

Knock, knock.

Who's There?

Uriah.

Uriah who?

Be sure to keep Uriah on the ball.

―Slam Dunk Amazing Fact―

The world's fastest motorcycle is the Suzuki GSX1300R Hayabusa. It has been clocked at 186 miles per hour.

A batter returned to the dugout after striking out for the third time in a row. He was so mad he kicked the bat rack.

"Hey, watch what you are doing," said the coach. "You could break a leg and then we would have trouble trading you to another team."

What is the name for a baseball player who falls
   asleep in the bullpen?
A bulldozer.

What has eighteen legs and catches flies?
A baseball team.

Reba: What's the very lowest game you can
   play?
Rene: I pass.
Reba: *Baseball*

Nit: Where is the largest diamond in the
   world found?
Wit: I have know idea.
Nit: On a baseball field.

Seth: Which baseball team do you like best, the Red Sox or the Nylons?

Kyler: The Red Sox.

Seth: But the Nylons get more runs.

—Slam Dunk Amazing Fact—

The world's fastest land vehicle is the Thrust SSC. On October 15, 1997, Andy Green drove the Thrust at an amazing speed of 763 miles per hour. It only took the jet-powered car five seconds to reach this speed.

Little Leaguer: Dad, what does a ballplayer do when his eyesight starts going bad?

Dad: He gets a job as an umpire.

Why did the boy take a ladder to the ball game?
Because he heard the Giants were playing.

Lambert: What was the outcome of the base-
ball game played on the Ark?
Laszlo: That's a mystery.
Lambert: A Noah-hitter.

Coach speaking to his baseball team: "Sure
we're behind in the game...but seven runs here,
and another nine runs there, and we'll be right
back in it."

Where is baseball mentioned in the Bible?

Genesis 1:1	In the Beginning (big inning)
Genesis 3:6	Eve stole first and Adam stole second
Genesis 24:15-16	Rebekah went to the well with a "pitcher."

Exodus 4:4	And he put forth his hand, and caught it.
Judges 17:7-20	When Gideon rattled the pitchers
Luke 15:11-32	The prodigal son made a home run

Slam Dunk Amazing Fact

The world's fastest boat is called the Spirit of Australia. This boat was driven by Ken Warby and hit speeds up to 317 miles per hour.

The Little League coach called one of his players over to him and said he would like to explain some of the principles of sportsmanship.

"We don't believe in temper tantrums or screaming at the umpires. We also do not use bad language or sulk when we lose. Do you understand what I am saying?"

The boy nodded.

"All right then," said the coach. "Do you think you can explain it to your father jumping around over there in the stands?"

Igor: What position do pigs play on a baseball team?
Theda: I have no idea.
Igor: Short-slop.

How can you make a fly ball?
Hit him with a bat.

Filbert: What happens when baseball players get old?
Freeda: I haven't a clue.
Filbert: They go batty.

Nit: What do you get if you cover a baseball field with sandpaper?

Wit: I don't have the foggiest.

Nit: A diamond in the rough.

—Slam Dunk Amazing Fact—

The man who scored the most points in his basketball career was Kareem Abdul-Jabbar. Kareem scored a total of 38,387 points.

Where should a baseball team never wear red?
In the bullpen.

A baseball fan is an individual who has the unique ability to sit 500 feet from home plate and see better than an umpire standing 5 feet away.

What famous baseball player drives bugs batty?
Mickey Mantis.

Why is a tent like a baseball?
Because they both have to be pitched.

There was an umpire who was famous for wandering all over the baseball diamond. During one game, he got hit on the head by a fly ball and fell down.

The catcher said, "We've just witnessed the fall of the roamin' umpire."

A baseball team scored six runs in one inning, but not one boy reached home. Why not?
Because it was a girl's team.

⚾ ⚾ ⚾

Slam Dunk Amazing Fact

The longest home run was hit by Mickey Mantle. His ball traveled 634 feet.

⚾ ⚾ ⚾

Baseball fans are a little crazy. They go to a ball game and then sing, "Take me out to the ball game."

⚾ ⚾ ⚾

Ichabod: What is the whitest part of a baseball park?

Ignatius: I give up.

Ichabod: The bleachers.

1st baseball player: Why did you switch from a 34-ounce bat to a 29-ounce bat?

2nd baseball player: Well, when I strike out, it's lighter to carry back to the bench.

Why is a game of baseball like a pancake?

Because they both need batters.

I was going to be a big league umpire, but they wouldn't let me. I kept passing the eye exam.

Slam Dunk Amazing Fact

The longest field goal that was kicked was by Tom Dempsey. He kicked the ball 63 yards.

Why did the man bring a rope to the baseball
 game?

To tie up the score.

Why does it take longer to run from second
 base to third base than it takes to run from
 first base to second base?

*Because there's a shortstop between second and
 third.*

What do you get if you cross a lizard with a
 baseball player?

An outfielder who catches flies with his tongue.

Kati: Why does a baseball pitcher raise one
 leg when he pitches?

Zelda: My mind is blank.

Kati: If he raised both legs, he would fall down.

Barnaby: What position would a midget play on your baseball team?

Bailey: You tell me.

Barnaby: Shortstop.

Slam Dunk Amazing Fact

Joseph Odhiambo holds the record for dribbling the most basketballs at the same time. He dribbled six balls at once.

Little Brother: Thanks for the baseball cards, but I can't read yet.

Big Brother: Don't worry. You can still look at the pitchers.

What is chocolate and is in the baseball Hall of Fame?

Babe Ruth.

Where is the headquarters of the Umpires' Association?

In the Umpire State Building.

How should a girl flirt with a baseball player?

Bat her eyelashes.

Why couldn't they sell soda pop at the double-header?

The home team lost the opener.

When does a baseball player wear armor?
When he has to play knight games.

⚾ ⚾ ⚾

—Slam Dunk Amazing Fact—

The man who scored the most world records in one day was Jesse Owens. He set six world records in 45 minutes. The records were set in the 100-yard dash, the long jump, the 220-yard race, the 200-meter race, the 220-yard low-hurdles, and the 200-meter hurdles.

⚾ ⚾ ⚾

Christy: Where does a baseball player live?
Clara: Beats me.
Christy: At home.

⚾ ⚾ ⚾

A father watched his young son practice baseball in the backyard by throwing the ball up and swinging at it. Time and time again the boy missed. All of a sudden the boy noticed that his father was watching. He turned and waved and said, "You see how great a pitcher I am?"

Gus: Why did the umpire throw the chicken out of the baseball game?

Gabriel: I have no idea.

Gus: He suspected fowl play.

Georgie: Have you ever seen a line drive?

Porgie: No, but I've seen a ball park.

Igor: What would you get if you crossed a lobster and a baseball player?

Theda: My mind is a blank.

Igor: A pinch hitter.

─Slam Dunk Amazing Fact─

The longest foot race occurred in 1929. It was from New York City to Los Angeles. It covered 3,635 miles and was won by Jonny Salo of Finland. It took him 525 hours and 57 minutes.

What was a spider doing on the baseball team?
Catching flies.

Delbert: Why couldn't Robin play baseball?
Darlene: I can't explain.
Delbert: He forgot his bat, man.

Willy: What happens when you hit a pop fly?

Nelly: I give up.

Willy: The same thing that happens when you hit a mom fly—the whole fly family gets mad.

Slam Dunk Amazing Fact

The fastest recorded speed on a skateboard was 78.37 miles per hour. The rider was lying down on the board. The fastest speed for someone standing up is held by Gary Hardwick. Gary traveled, standing up, at the amazing speed of 62.55 miles per hour.

15

Hunting

What is the difference between a hunter and a fisherman?

A hunter lies in wait while the fisherman waits and lies.

🐾🐾 🐾🐾

George and Harry got lost in the woods while on a hunting trip. George said to Harry, "Don't worry. All we have to do is shoot into the air three times, stay where we are, and someone will find us."

They shot into the air, but no one came. They waited for a while and tried it again. Still no one came.

Harry said to George, "This better work this time. We're down to our last three arrows."

Game Warden: Have you ever hunted bear?
Tourist: No, but I've gone water skiing in my shorts.

Clayton: Why did the big-game hunter give up hunting for elephants?
Owen: I don't know.
Clayton: He got tired of carrying around the decoys.

There are two kinds of hunters—those who hunt for sport and those who catch something.

──Slam Dunk Amazing Fact──

The highest air on a skateboard was 16 feet 6 inches.

It was hunting season when a state trooper walked up to a man and his son and said, "That's a nice buck you have on the top of your car."

The surprised man couldn't say anything, so his little boy answered for him, "That's nothing! You should see the one we have in the trunk!"

Knock, knock.

Who's there?

Ron.

Ron who?

Ron fast. Here comes a wild tiger.

Talkative hunter: Once while I was having a meal in the jungle, a lion came so close to me that I could feel his breath on the back of my neck. What did I do?

Bored listener: Turn your collar up?

Sportsman: Is there any good hunting in these parts?

Native: Sure, there's plenty of hunting but very little finding.

Slam Dunk Amazing Fact

The longest skateboard jump was recorded at a distance of 56 feet.

Two hunters had been out several hours and one of them had been growing uneasy. Finally panic overtook him. "Were lost!" he cried to his companion. "What shall we do?"

"Keep your shirt on!" said his companion. "Shoot an extra deer and the game warden will be here in a minute and a half."

Petula: What steps should you take if a tiger charges you?

Olaf: Long ones.

"When I was in India," said the club bore, "I saw a tiger come down to the water where some women were washing clothes. It was a very fierce tiger, but one woman, with great presence of mind, splashed some water in its face and it ran away."

"Gentlemen," said a man in an armchair, "I can vouch for the truth of his story. Some minutes after this incident, I was coming to the water. I met this tiger, and, as is my habit, stroked its whiskers. Gentlemen, those whiskers were wet."

🐾🐾 🐾🐾

─Slam Dunk Amazing Fact─

The longest free fall was done by Joseph Kittinger. He lept out of a balloon at 102,800 feet in the air and fell a distance of 84,715 feet.

16

Coaches

1st reporter: If you were the coach, how would you have played the final quarter of the last play-off game?

2nd reporter: Under an assumed name.

A coach is a man who will gladly lay down your life for the team.

Reporter: Coach, how would you sum up your
    swim team's record this last season?

Coach: Nobody drowned.

You can guess that your job as a coach is in
trouble when the booster club gives you a gift
certificate to the U-Haul company.

Reporter: Could you comment on what it's like
    to be a track coach?

Coach: It is simple. All you have to say is,
    "Okay boys, keep to the left and get back
    as soon as you can."

Our coach is very kind to the referees. He
helps them feel their way into the gym before
the games.

—Slam Dunk Amazing Fact—

Bill Knox bowled a perfect game of 300 points. He wanted to prove to everyone that it could be done by rolling the ball on a certain spot each time. This is called "spot bowling."

"What's so special about that," you may ask? "Haven't other bowlers bowled a perfect score?" The answer is yes, they have—but not the way Bill Knox did.

Bill had two of the pin boys hold up a screen about one foot above the foul line. This blocked his vision of the alley and the pins. Bill bowled a perfect ball each time without seeing the pins.

Is it true that a fat coach keeps his players in good condition by having them run laps around him?

Reporter: Coach, how do you prepare your players for the crowd noise they will hear during the game?

Coach: I play a laugh track.

Reporter: How can a coach know that his job is in jeopardy?

Coach: When you see the marching band form a noose at halftime.

Reporter: What does a coach say to his team when they lose 20 straight games in a row?

Coach: Nice sweating, fellas. Way to shower, men.

Reporter: Is it true that you send cards to all of the referees?

Coach: Yes, it is. They're in braille so they can read them.

──Slam Dunk Amazing Fact──

The longest bungee jump was done by Jochen Schweizer. His 3,320-foot bungee leap was done out of a helicopter.

17

Scrambled Sports

Here's a scramble with letters to sort. The right answer is a type of sport.

Llabaseb

Here's a scramble with letters to sort. The right answer is a type of sport.

Nisetn

Here's a scramble with letters to sort. The right answer is a type of sport.

Ufrsgni

Here's a scramble with letters to sort. The right answer is a type of sport.

Dshuelroabff

Here's a scramble with letters to sort. The right answer is a type of sport.

Eginocna

Here's a scramble with letters to sort. The right answer is a type of sport.

Yksgnivid

Slam Dunk Amazing Fact

Jon Kretchman holds the longest barefoot water-ski jump. He traveled a distance of 84.6 feet.

Here's a scramble with letters to sort. The right answer is a type of sport.

Cstiaborca

Here's a scramble with letters to sort. The right answer is a type of sport.

Yrarche

Here's a scramble with letters to sort. The right answer is a type of sport.

Nbdmtioan

Here's a scramble with letters to sort. The right answer is a type of sport.

Kghiin

—Slam Dunk Amazing Fact—

The fastest snowboarder was Darren Powell. He got up to the speed of 125.44 miles per hour.

18

Golf

Why did the golfer wear an extra pair of trousers?
In case he got a hole in one.

Where do golfers go to dance?
To the golf ball.

Mr. Wilson: Caddy, why didn't you see where that ball went?

Caddy: Well, it doesn't usually go anywhere, Mr. Wilson. You caught me off guard.

The other day I was playing golf and saw a strange thing. A golfer got mad at how he was playing and tossed his bag of clubs into the lake. A few minutes later I saw him wade into the lake and search for his golf bag. He found the bag, unzipped one of the pockets, and took out his car keys—then he threw the clubs back in the water.

Two men were beginning a game of golf. The first man stepped up to the tee and his first drive gave him a hole-in-one. The second man stepped up to the tee and said, "Okay, now I'll take my practice swing, and then we'll start the game."

Bertram: Playing golf must be bad for your heart.

Bunsby: What makes you say that?

Bertram: I just heard a golfer say he had four strokes on the very first hole.

┌─ **Slam Dunk Amazing Fact** ─┐

Martinus Juiper put on his skates and skated 339.68 miles in 24 hours.

When you putt well on the golf course, you are a good putter. But when the other fellow is putting well, he has a good putter.

Golfer: If you laugh at me again when I hit the ball, I'll knock your block off.

Caddy: You wouldn't even know what club to use.

Golfer: You must be the world's worst caddy!

Caddy: No, sir. That would be too much of a coincidence.

I have a friend who has benefited from playing golf. His golf game has made him an expert in the field of wilderness survival.

Teacher: Remember what happens to boys who use bad language when they play marbles.

Boy: Yep, teacher, they grow up to play golf.

Teacher: Remember what happens to boys who use bad language when they play marbles.

1st golfer: Why don't you play golf with George anymore?

2nd golfer: Would you play with someone who puts down the wrong score and moves the ball when you're not watching?

1st golfer: No, I wouldn't.

2nd golfer: Well, neither will George.

─Slam Dunk Amazing Fact─

Have you ever gotten dizzy? Neil Wilson spun 60 rotations in a row on his ice skates.

Golf is a long walk that is filled with frustration and creative arithmetic.

Golfer: This is terrible. I've never played this badly before.

Caddy: Oh, then you have played before?

Reginald: Why didn't the golfer wear two shoes?

Bartholomew: I don't have the foggiest.

Reginald: Because he had a hole in one.

What do you get if you hit a gopher with a golf ball?

A mole-in-one.

1st golfer: What's your golf score?

2nd golfer: Well, not so good. It's 72.

1st golfer: That's not so bad. In fact, it's really good.

2nd golfer: Well, I'm hoping I do better on the next hole.

Ben: What has two legs, two arms, and goes put, put, put, put, put?

Len: That's a mystery.

Ben: A very poor golfer.

─**Slam Dunk Amazing Fact**─

Jackie Bellinger and Lisa Lomas Bellinger hit a Ping-Pong ball back and forth 173 times in one minute.

Golfer: Why do you keep looking at your watch?

Caddy: This isn't a watch, sir. It's a compass.

Golfer: How would you have played that last shot, caddy?

Caddy: Under an assumed name.

I was three-over today. One over a house, one over a patio, and one over a swimming pool.

Golfer: Caddy, how do you think I could
    improve my golf game?

Caddy: Your trouble is that you stand too close
    to the ball...after you've hit it.

    My golf game is improving. Yesterday I hit
the ball in one.

Golfer: Notice any improvement since last
    year?

Caddy: Polished your clubs, didn't you?

Bill: I'd move heaven and earth to break my
    100 score.

Phil: Try moving heaven. You've already moved
    plenty of earth today.

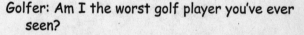

—Slam Dunk Amazing Fact—

The heaviest athlete is Emmanuel "Manny" Yarborough. He is 6' 8" inches tall and weighs 604 pounds.

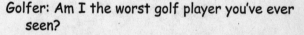

Golfer: Am I the worst golf player you've ever seen?

Caddy: I wouldn't say you were the worst golfer I have seen on this course—but I have seen places today that I've never seen before.

1st golfer: I can't see why you play golf with him. He's a bad loser.

2nd golfer: I'd rather play with a bad loser than a winner any time.

Golfer: My doctor says I can't play golf.
Caddy: Oh, he's played with you too, huh?

I asked the golf professional how I could get greater distance on my drive. He said, "Simple. Just hit the ball and jump backward."

What is the biggest handicap in golf?
Honesty.

19

Jogging

Wife: Harry, let's go jogging together.

Husband: Why?

Wife: My doctor told me I could lose weight by working out with a dumbbell.

I know a guy who belongs to Joggers Anonymous. When he gets the urge to jog he calls a friend. The friend brings over a pizza and a banana split, and they eat till the urge passes.

Ken: There's nothing like getting up at five in the morning, taking an ice-cold shower, and jogging five miles before breakfast.

Bob: How long have you been doing this?

Ken: I start tomorrow.

Joe: I go jogging every day.

Moe: How fast do you run?

Joe: Not very fast. I got arrested for loitering.

──Slam Dunk Amazing Fact──

Charles Linster was not very big. He was only 5′ 6.5″ tall. He only weighed 153 pounds. He was 16 years of age when he asked his coaches at the New Trier High School in Winnetka, Illinois to act as his witnesses.

The date was October 7, 1965. For the next 3 hours and 54 minutes, Charles Linster executed 6,006 push-ups without stopping.

I don't go jogging for 30 minutes just to increase my pulse rate. I can get the same thing accomplished by looking at my wife's shopping bills.

Why did the man with amnesia take up running?
He wanted to jog his memory.

I was going to go jogging this morning but I strained my back when I put on my running shoes.

1st Jogger: Do you like to jog?
2nd Jogger: I used to.
1st Jogger: What do you mean, used to?
2nd Jogger: It's too embarrassing. The last time I went out for a run, my neighbor asked me if he could walk along with me.

Since jogging came along, more and more people are collapsing in perfect health.

Slam Dunk Amazing Fact

Steve McPeak rode a unicycle that was 32-feet tall from Chicago to Los Angeles. That's a three-story building high.

Did you hear about the runner in a marathon? He was last out of 3,000 people. It was a bad race that the person in front of him was making fun of him.

The second-to-last runner said, "How does it feel to come in last?"

The runner at the very end of the line said, "I don't know. Why don't you tell me." And then he dropped out of the race.

Things to do before you go jogging:
1.   Go to your cardiologist to have your heart examined.
2.   Go to your podiatrist to have your feet examined.
3.   Go to your psychiatrist and have your head examined.

Anybody who says they run 20 miles a day with their muscles stretching, their legs pounding, their hearts beating like a drum, and their lungs on fire because it makes them feel great will lie about everything else, too.

There is a very critical spot in a marathon. Just before you get to that spot—you are afraid you'll die. After you pass that spot, you are afraid you won't die.

My doctor told me that jogging could add years to my life. I took his advice and went jogging. I found out that he is right. I already feel 15 years older.

The reason I jog is because I just want to have a stomach that stops when I do.

20

Exercise

I always do my exercises regularly in the morning. Immediately after waking I sternly say to myself, "Ready, now up. Down. Up. Down!" And after two strenuous minutes I tell myself, "Okay, boy. Now try the other eyelid."

They say that exercise kills germs. Have you ever wondered how they get them to exercise?

It's important to remember when exercising, start slowly and then gradually taper off.

The only exercise some people get is jumping to conclusions, running down their friends, side-stepping responsibility, and pushing their luck.

Exercise is a feeling that will go away if you just lie down for a little while.

Clayton: Do you exercise daily?
Owen: No, Daley can exercise himself.

Slam Dunk Amazing Fact

William T. Mello holds the record for the most push-ups in one minute. He did an incredible 138 push-ups in one minute.

My wife's idea of exercise is to shop faster.

A physical fitness trainer is a person who lives off the fat of the land.

21

Hockey

Filbert: What do you do with a green hockey
  player?
Freeda: I don't know.
Filbert: Wait until he ripens.

I went to the fights the other night and a
hockey game broke out.

Ryan: How does a hockey player kiss?

Tyler: I couldn't guess.

Ryan: He puckers up.

—Slam Dunk Amazing Fact—

Wilt Chamberlain was the first man to score 100 points in a basketball game. This took place in 1962 when he played against the New York Knicks.

I took my children to the fights the other night. It was the first time they had ever seen an ice hockey game.

What are four different places where you can play the game of hockey?

On a field, on ice, underwater, or on a roller rink.

I've heard it said that there are three ways to play hockey: rough, rougher, and, "I'll help you find your teeth if you help me find mine."

Why did the hockey player color his teeth orange?

So they'd be easier to find on the ice.

22

Scrambled Sports

Here's a scramble with letters to sort. The right answer is a type of sport.

Ugtninh

Here's a scramble with letters to sort. The right answer is a type of sport.

Erllor ktasgin

Here's a scramble with letters to sort. The right answer is a type of sport.

Ybgur

Here's a scramble with letters to sort. The right answer is a type of sport.

Estwrgnil

Here's a scramble with letters to sort. The right answer is a type of sport.

Yvlloelabl

Slam Dunk Amazing Fact

The game of golf dates back to at least 1457. It is believed that the first game was played in Scotland.

Here's a scramble with letters to sort. The right answer is a type of sport.

Ersoh arngic

Here's a scramble with letters to sort. The right answer is a type of sport.

Oudj

Here's a scramble with letters to sort. The right answer is a type of sport.

Twaer oolp

Here's a scramble with letters to sort. The right answer is a type of sport.

Niks viingd

23

Sports Fans

A man was driving down the freeway when all of a sudden he looked out his right window and saw a man on a racing bicycle, pedaling furiously as he passed him. The driver of the car stepped on the gas and went faster and passed the man on the racing bicycle.

In just a moment, the man on the bicycle passed the car again. This time the driver of the car went even faster. Again the man on the bicycle passed the car.

Finally, the driver of the car stopped. The man on the racing bicycle also stopped alongside the right window. The driver of the car rolled down the window.

"Thank goodness you've stopped," said the man on the racing bicycle. "I had my suspenders caught in your back bumper."

Hubert: What contains more feet in winter than in summer?
Erastus: Who knows.
Hubert: An ice skating rink.

What is a mosquito's favorite sport?
Skin diving.

What is the best food for weight lifters to eat?
Mussels.

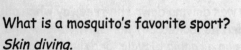

Did you hear about the athlete who finally got his letter from the coach? The letter said, "Why don't you try out for the croquet team."

——Slam Dunk Amazing Fact——

The largest soccer stadium in the world is found in Rio de Janeiro, Brazil. It holds 200,000 spectators.

Alfreda: How do acrobats fall in love?
Amelia: That's a mystery.
Alfreda: Head over heels.

If a tie is like kissing your sister, then losing is like kissing your mother-in-law with her teeth out.

When can you jump while sitting down?
While playing checkers.

Cornelius: What is incredibly intelligent,
weighs 200 pounds, and is made out of
iron?
Claudia: You tell me.
Cornelius: Albert Einstein Dumbbell.

Ski jumping is where you race down a steep
hill and fly 300 feet through the air. There has
to be a better way to meet nurses.

──Slam Dunk Amazing Fact──

December 11–12, 1999—Suresh Joachim
ran 78.71 miles carrying a ten-pound brick.

Millions of people play soccer because that way
they don't have to watch it on TV.

A small girl watching a water-skier said to her
father, "That man is silly. He'll never catch that
boat."

Skiing is a great sport, but there must be a
cheaper way to break bones.

I know a man that had to give up his sports announcing job. He was a play-by-play man for Ping-Pong matches.

What swimming stroke has the name of an insect?

The butterfly.

I don't ski. I refuse to participate in any sport that has an ambulance waiting at the bottom of the hill.

—Slam Dunk Amazing Fact—

American football has 12 times more injuries than basketball. Most injuries in basketball are to the knees.

What is another name for surfing?
A tide ride.

Ski pants come in three sizes. Small, medium, and don't bend over.

He was an excellent water-polo player until his horse drowned.

─Slam Dunk Amazing Fact─

The strangest sport is Russian "face slapping." It started when Wasyl Bezbordny and Michalko Toniusz stood face-to-face and then proceeded to slap each other's face. This continued for 30 hours until their friends realized that neither man would give up and made them stop.

Pam: How do you help an alligator on the football team who is very tired?

Melba: I give up.

Pam: Give it some Gator Aid.

Nit: Bullfighting is the number-one sport in Latin America.

Wit: That's revolting!

Nit: No, that's the number-two sport.

What do you call a boomerang that doesn't come back?

A stick.

Who are the most indispensable men in international soccer matches?

The riot police.

Carmen: What is a cow's favorite Olympic event?

Cordelia: I couldn't guess.

Carmen: The hurdles.

Did you hear about the athlete who was so dumb that when he earned his varsity letter somebody had to read it to him?

I wasn't much of an athlete in college, but I was the waterboy for the swim team.

Rowing has to be the worst sport. You sit down while playing and go backward to win.

Rudolf: What kind of ice skates wear out fast?
Wilbur: Beats me.
Rudolf: Cheapskates.

—Slam Dunk Amazing Fact—

Do you like riding bikes? How about a one-wheeled bike called a unicycle? This is a little more difficult.

In 1934, Walter Nilsson (a vaudeville performer) rode his unicycle across the United States. He started in New York and rode to San Francisco, California. It took him 117 days to ride his 8.5 foot unicycle 3,306 miles.

24

Answers to
Scrambled Sports

PAGES 31-34

Sorcs-rynutco nsikig	Cross-country skiing
Ismwgnim	Swimming
Sheohsroes	Horseshoes
Tkrca nda lefid	Track and field
Ghweit gliiftn	Weight lifting
Ngfenci	Fencing
Logf	Golf
Gihh mupijng	High jumping
Derdnuh dyar sahd	Hundred yard dash
Tsoh upt	Shot put

PAGES 79-82

Idefl yekoch	Field hockey
Wginobl	Bowling
Quorcet	Croquet
Lloofabt	Football
Oopl	Polo
Lldnahba	Handball
Xiobng	Boxing
Tgilnrwes	Wrestling
Wsginimm	Swimming
Klalbetsab	Basketball

PAGES 113-116

Llabaseb	Baseball
Nisetn	Tennis
Ufrsgni	Surfing
Dshuelroaff	Shuffleboard
Eginocna	Canoeing
Yksgnivid	Skydiving
Cstiaborca	Acrobatics
Yrarche	Archery
Nbdmtioan	Badminton
Kghiin	Hiking

PAGES 141-144

Ugtninh	Hunting
Erllor ktasgin	Roller skating
Ybgur	Rugby
Estwrgnil	Wrestling
Yvlloelabl	Volleyball
Ersoh arngic	Horse racing
Oudj	Judo
Twaer oolp	Water polo
Niks viingd	Skin diving